WITHDRAWN
UTSA LIBRARIES

P9-ECJ-531

BOOKS IN PRINT BY DAVID KHERDIAN

Macmillan Publishing Co., Inc.

*Settling America: the Ethnic Expression of 14
   Contemporary Poets*
Visions of America: by the Poets of Our Time
The Nonny Poems

The Giligia Press

Six San Francisco Poets
On the Death of My Father and Other Poems
Down at the Santa Fe Depot: 20 Fresno Poets
Homage to Adana
Looking Over Hills

The Nonny Poems

The Nonny Poems

BY DAVID KHERDIAN

MACMILLAN PUBLISHING CO., INC.
NEW YORK

COLLIER MACMILLAN PUBLISHERS
LONDON

Copyright © 1974 by David Kherdian

All rights reserved. No part of this book may be reproduced
or transmitted in any form or by any means, electronic or
mechanical, including photocopying, recording or by any
information storage and retrieval system, without permission
in writing from the Publisher.

Macmillan Publishing Co., Inc.
866 Third Avenue, New York, N.Y. 10022
Collier-Macmillan Canada Ltd.

Library of Congress Cataloging in Publication Data
Kherdian, David.
   The Nonny poems.
   I. Title.
PS3561.H4N6   811'.5'4   73-11832
ISBN 0-02-562990-5

First Printing 1974

Printed in the United States of America

LIBRARY
University of Texas
At San Antonio

ACKNOWLEDGMENTS

The second stanza of "To Nonny" was first published in *The Horn Book Magazine* (August 1972) within the article "Nonny Hogrogian" by D.K.

"The First Day," "To Nonny," "Of Husbands and Wives," "Last Night," "The Portraits," "You and I and the Brothers Grimm," "In Our Time," and "The Subway Encounter" originally appeared in *The Lamp in the Spine*, together with a drawing of the poet by Nonny Hogrogian. "Getting Married" and "The First Day" are reprinted from *Prairie Schooner*. Copyright © 1973 by the University of Nebraska Press.

Other poems have appeared in *Granite*, *Prairie Schooner*, *riverrun*, *Café Solo*, *Schist*, *Ararat*, *Avarayr*, and as broadsides by the Phineas Press and The Giligia Press.

The anthologies NORTHERN LIGHTS and OUR PLACE have also published poems.

To the editors of these books, magazines and little presses, grateful thanks.

CONTENTS

New York

New Hampshire

New York

THE FIRST DAY

We had lunch with white
wine and cheese. I brought
that; you made the soup.
Armenian olives and bread.
And the *mezas* you served
in small Oriental bowls.

When it was done, and after
we had talked, I put on my
hat and then removed it at
the door to give you a
parting hug and kiss on
the cheek.

First hours, then days
later I began to realize
that nothing is as casual
as that for which the end
is not yet written.

2.14.71

NONNY

While I imagine that I am
about to write this poem,
I also imagine that you
have begun a new drawing
for your book. And as the
form of it begins to come
into existence in my mind,
I realize that it is your
face I am drawing with these
unformed words. With memories.
With images I cannot seize
or hold. We hardly know each
other; we just recently met.
Yet I am longing for you as
if we were lovers.

2.14.71

THE IDEA

I like the idea of your being
Nonny Hogrogian.
Walking down the street,
black coat on; orange, rust-
brown jumper. Oh, your shoes.
You stop at a store window
for the reflection given back.
Then turning, stepping,
(held by this secret embrace)
you are walking,
walking through magic
into this turning year.

2.16.71

You say, are you tired; would you
like to sleep? And then scouch down
and fit yourself beneath my enveloping
arm, for you know already the position
we will take for sleep. If I move, I
find you turning as I turn. Whatever
occurs, you are ready in advance: more
love, a kiss—whatever is happening,
you make it happen right.

This is our first night together, but
already you know how the marriage
bed lies.

2.17.71

While you fidgeted by my side
(a strange body beside yours in
sleep), you were suddenly tossed
into the angry words of your
mother: who came, you thought,
to carry you away from our bed
of love.

When I turned against you and
that tide, that threatened to
take you from my side, we awoke
together into each other's eyes,
and I held you trembling and
crying until you named your fear.

2.17.71

FOR YOU

I am turned on my side, arm
crooked and under my head;
legs crunched up and writing
with my right hand. This paper,
before I started writing, seemed
as cold as my room and as empty
as my life now feels without you,
and so I am beckoning you with
these black markings, which are
the scratchings of time that
your absence has left.

2.18.71

TO NONNY

There is a green light cast from
your hanging window plants that
pours over your shoulder as you work.

You are murmuring and sighing, and
I am imagining the drawing that is
moving down through the tributaries of
your body into your arm and down through
your fingertips onto the paper that
is lit by your face.

I want to sit here with my back to
you for just one more moment, to
enjoy these thoughts of you, before
getting up and writing down the quiet
of what has taken place.

2.28.71

NONNY YOUR SHOES

O your tanned low-heeled shoes,
that wear at the toes your faintly
blushed & rosy cheeks, sit and stare
out at me from beside the chair,
beside your bed, that I sit and
write on while you are away—over
into the next room, where you are
making a drawing that will, if
I am lucky, be as lovely
as your feet.

3.2.71

AH, NONNY, NONNY

From far away somewhere you bring
your red long-nozzled watering can
from the kitchen and begin pouring
water from yourself to your plants.

Talking to the first one and then
murmuring to each of the rest, you
move around your little apartment
on naked sunny feet.

They know your red long-nozzled
watering can and have adjusted long
ago to this cramped city life, but
what must they think of my masculine
presence in this creatively ordered
until now feminine house.

3.2.71

THE WAIT

I have never before been taken so close
to the idea of death—the fear of failing
health, of accident—or that there might
be some cosmic law that would declare our
love a mistaken intent.

When you left tonight for your class, I
had to lie down, to feel through to myself
from this altered posture, and to look at
my life in this way from within the eyes
of your walls and your plants.

If your plants speak to me, if your walls
talk to me, you must come and tell me
their message, as I also wait on your
feminine patience to calm this man fear.

3.3.71

LAST NIGHT

We awoke into the day from out of each
other's arms. Last night, for the first
time, you said you were moved by the
arms that held you in love into the arms
that awaited your sleep. Softened by our
faith, hushed by this trust, we stayed
all day in this single room, and made
our work within the moving noises of
our private lives. By night we knew that
the life that is stroked into existence
by the forms of art is the poem that is
brushed into being by the grace of love.

3.3.71

The shape of my Armenian nose is slowly
becoming the distorted shape of the noses
for the figures you are drawing for your
book of tales from the pen of Grimm. The
mustache on the old flounder catcher from
the tale "The Fisherman and His Wife" is
also mine—and all the women seem to have
your funny nose (seemingly connected to
your eyebrows in a mask) and your upturned
innocent mouth that smiles.

Through my poems, through your art, we are
re-creating the race in an image that is ours.
The gentleness of my art, the tenderness of
yours, were there long before we met, so will
not go away—because it was for a time such
as this that we held our faith.

3.3.71

Last night we went through the hell again
of the ill will of our families, who still
find it difficult to accept our happiness
and to believe in our love.

Because I wanted to be alone to think,
you left the house and went to your
class—but after you had gone, I watched
the clock and played sad songs on the
phonograph until you came back.

Later we talked, and then you cried and
I laughed in a kind of mutual release,
until exhausted we plunged ourselves
into the deep dreams and desires of our
bodies—but nothing would help.

And then, this morning, you dressed yourself
in blues and blacks that complemented your
greying hair, but it only made me feel
that we had grown old and sad, until I
realized it is only the clothes we wear
to weather the world when we are driven to
compromise because of the world's despair.

3.4.71

This evening's Armenian meal that you
cooked with pine nuts and strange
spices unknown to me, helped carry me
over from the food of my family to the
food of yours—the gentle journey a man
makes when he takes a wife: and afterwards
you drew me for the first time, squinting
beautifully for perspective and giving
me a new glimpse into the changing beauty
caused by our growing love, as my own
severe pose for you gave you a new look
into an aspect of my character you said
you had never seen before.

3.4.71

THE PORTRAITS

The plants are breathing as you work.
On each side of the ones that hang
from the ceiling and rest on the sill
are two early portraits you did in
oils from a time before I was ever
here. Sitting in quiet, my back to
you as you work at your table, I slowly
begin to focus all these parts of your
life into a gentle music that travels
before my eyes from out of my ears,
and that is being punctuated by the
scratchings you make on paper as you
begin a new drawing from out of your
own evolving sphere.

3.4.71

It has taken all this time to accept
the new emotion our love has called up;
to meet the fear we have tried to avoid
of an interfering world—and then,
finally, to move ourselves out of each
other and to travel back together again
(in a singular motion) towards some
unknown but awaiting end—that has
finally given way to this evening's
quiet hour, to the beat of its own
normal and unpossessing demands.

And so, come 5:30, I sit here and write
and smell the same aroma I have known
from all the years going back, and I
know there will be pilaf and eggplant
from my new girl, who has taken over
from where our earlier lives had come
to an end.

3.5–6.71

YOU AND I AND THE BROTHERS GRIMM

It's noon now and you have gone out
for sandwiches, leaving me alone with
the presence of you that will soon begin
to emerge from this paper as I write.
Last night, after long absence, I returned
again and ate with you the food you had
prepared in the hope that it was being
made for the two of us, and then we went
to bed early and knew fully for the first
time the ecstasy that uniting brings, when
the body, holding its breath in wait,
exhales its love each to each; and then
rising from that glow while I slept, you
made your last drawing for your book from
Grimm, which I am looking at now for the
first time: a wedding scene in which the
bride holds in her heart the ecstasy of
our hour, while her face tells the fictive
tale of another's art. But only you and I
know that the crooked nose above the
mustache of the man wearing a crown—as
he looks down on her protectively from
above—belongs to the man in the bed you
had then just come from.

3.13.71

THE HOUR

At my back you sit hunched
over your worktable, carving
lovebirds into the waxed
molds of our wedding rings.

"Coming out to be silly
birds," you say.
"Quiet, I'm writing,"
I reply.

Earlier we had talked about
how easy our work had been
going in the weeks since we
met; and now, thinking back
on all of it, I can scarcely
believe that a line I had
written into one of my earliest
poems to you, will be engraved,
as your choice, on the inside
of the rings you are carving
now as I write—

in just four days
when the inevitable time
of our short long wait
will have come to an end
and we will have become
each other's life.

3.13.71

My cruelty that you said would never show
itself to you revealed itself this morning
in bed when I teased your body, causing you
to cry in shame and regret. I didn't know at
first what I was doing—and you wouldn't
admit to yourself what I had done: that the
game was not fun but the serious ugly fight
each couple wages when the stakes are love,
because the loss (and the fear because of
vulnerability) is hate. Am I right to think
it won't happen again, that I have finally
seen for the first time the sadistic side
of my own nature, and that the desire not to
fail in your eyes will eventually improve
who I am? If I am to beg your forgiveness
in a poem, can I say now that the mouse that
runs up to your navel, knocks to enter and
is denied, is the now accepted wisp of
transplanted life our ancestors carried with
them from the other side, when we were one
race and incest was something no one knew
or feared; that your large Armenian breasts
are feeding stations for the young we hope
will come along. Not very funny images,
perhaps, or very good poetry, but they say,
though they say it poorly, that I accept
who we are, where we came from, the time we
live in, and what I hope we can do with the
future that is ours.

3.14.71

THE VISITORS

Today I met your former lover—the
shy and boyish man from downstairs
who came up with his two Rhodesian
dogs (gentle monsters caged by the
invisible bars of this doomed city)
to lend us his typewriter and to
have a drink; and while we talked
of nothing, I noticed without looking
the gentle way in which you deferred
to me and were concerned with the
way I handled myself in the company
of another man—and I knew what I
hadn't had to think of before, that
in experiencing me with others you
were also experiencing for the first
time important aspects of your
womanhood that had never before come
to the surface, but had now, suddenly,
become a part of this new self,
because it was held in its becoming
by my strength.

                    3.14.71

GETTING MARRIED

Walking across Third Avenue, up from the
subway, and on our way home from the
license bureau and the tensions of
that and the day, we moved along
without speaking while you held tightly
to my waist, because you felt yourself
drifting away out of fear and fright.
And staring into your eyes when I knew
they could not focus on mine, I
deliberately shouted, "Getting married,"
to startle you because I knew it would
make you jump—and the look you gave
I have kept, because it carried up from
all the gone years your innocent youth,
and told me in a flash all that I had won.

3.15.71

THE SUBWAY ENCOUNTER

I'm just remembering that coming home on
the subway yesterday afternoon from the
license bureau, I saw our images—for
the first time as a couple—on the window
across from where we sat. The shock of
the upcoming marriage had made you pensive,
caused you to withdraw, and you had a
strangely childlike look, despite your
greying hair and worried face—while I
had the typical open-eyed, immovable
stare of a man in shock. Still, I was
able to look at us as a pair: or rather,
I could feel myself looking at the strange
Armenian couple in the window across from
us and was able to consider them something
other than strangers. But we not only did
not look like *us* at that moment, or like
a pair, a couple or a match—or anything
else that suggested mutual movement,
accord, or travelers in time. But then
we are not the branded or the damned (as
so many couples who look like couples are),
but two strangers, who became friends and
then lovers—just these happy, frightened,
pleased to do time together, misplaced
Armenians in a strangely foreign land.

3.16.71

The marriage day has come and now is
nearly gone. From the start it scuttled
along like the subway that took us to
City Hall, all out of whack with the
rhythms we had come to know and rely
upon as our own. Barbara, our witness,
brought a rose, that now sits a stranger
among your simple green plants; and
your lawyer sent champagne, which we
had with dinner instead of one of the
wines we like. And tonight we addressed
our poem/drawing wedding announcements,
and now I will go out to mail them,
while you stay home to do the dishes.
But something has been seized and
carried from out of this hour—we can
go forward now as ourselves, for
ourselves, and tomorrow the first leg
of our long journey begins, when we
leave this foolishly monumental and
stupid city and begin in another
place our own quiet
country lives.

3.17.71

New Hampshire

WINTER, NEW HAMPSHIRE

1/

chickadees
round suet balls
winter has come

2/

late day
sun sets
on moose mountain
dark cold
blue sky
deer are moving
on evening's
quiet shoulders

shadowless earth

invisible orion
in the sky

3/

birds in suet
sad wintry song
late day
snow banks the
apple trees
haze down
moose mountain
december fog
drifts
by our window
into sight

4/

snow clouds
slowly lift
off moose mountain

the powdery
snow in their
wake
dust the pines
above the meadow

everything
in all directions
green white brown

5/

white plains
in forest grove
snowshoe tracks
round
pine trees
pass & go

dog barks
off further
hills
echo me home

6/

early morning
snow shadows
blue
clouds bank
the sun
on moose mountain
deer tracks
lead away
& into
my life

THE SECOND POEM

Outside
cats are jumping
from real or
imagined butterfly
shadows—
birds circling
suet balls
are spooked
by their own
motion and
fiery appetites

Inside
hushed, motionless
I believe
again in the
salvation of
my poetry
and write

WAITING FOR BIRDS

two day old
seed-filled bird
feeder
hanging from
the porch—
having birds come
fills our home
with what is
outside
our home:
as much
a part of our lives
as the furniture
we sit in
food we eat
books we write
waiting
waiting for the birds to come

THE POEM

I am engaged
in making
such books
these poems
for my wife
& life
our animals
and home

moose mountain
& bear hill
before and
in back
tomorrow &
the days gone

I am rescuing
the years
and who will say
that this
obscurity
is not my joy
that I should
not be content
to make such
forms
from out of this
borrowed life

AFTER SUPPER

a little cognac
after supper
in the comfy chair
with Nonny
lying easy
on the couch
Sato sprawled
across her lap
while mongoose nose
rabbit back ears
Bujo
bites her toes
& growls

THE KISS

Bujo
with his big
fat buddha belly
runs across the
room
stops
and kisses Sato
by touching his
nose to hers

and sniffing

what should
I guess it
means
nothing
I am here
it just happened
it is a
small happiness

cup your hands
they will hold
this poem

HEY NONNY

the chickadee
must have seen
a seed
in the snow
down
from the branch
to go neck
deep into the
soft white
of it
& now
the snow is
falling
on his head

THE ROBYS

a family of four
walking up the
path beyond our
house
David is pulling
his son on a sled
Barbara in back
is calling to Jennifer
up in front
they are many colors
the snow is white
the background trees
are green & brown
lips and branches
legs and arms
are moving
from our invisible
window
their voices do
not make a sound

RETURNING

as Sato calls
from beneath
the window
to Bujo
or her own
frustration

he only looks
down from
his chair
points his
nose at the
floor
and ignores
her female
alarm

THE ONLY SUN WE'VE SEEN ALL DAY

the messenger gold
beak of the male
grosbeak
beneath the pines
& the downy dust-
brown female grosbeak
at his side
all around them & through
the day it snowed
and all day we waited
at the window
in confusion & want

YOU

cats among holly
leaves
playing & fighting
you in my
papa chair
writing a story
for children
to read
and delight in

over here
on the couch
sprawled
blanket spread
over my tired
body
I survey my life

room filled
with Christmas
last year
new years
coming and gone

24:II:72

pushing heavy
breasted through
the snow
hurriedly pecking
at fallen seeds
he makes a
zigzag trail through
the half-buried
prickly pine

now
looking up
he's gone
the only ruby-
crowned kinglet
this winter
hurrah!

LIVING IN QUIET

tit man
Bujo
sucking on
his blanket
slurp slurp
these noises
are his poem
& this scratching
of pen on paper
our sound
together
we are here
living in a kind
of quiet
we are here
with all that
we needed
never got
are getting
and will hold
against the time
to come

26:III:72

early evening
late supper
on the stove
I lay waiting
on the couch
reading Reznikoff
about an earlier
America and
his Israel of
fact & fiction
on the porch
the unnamed raccoon
eats his way
across a dish
of crumbs

POEM FOR NONNY

blanket lazily thrown
over your legs
late evening
night quiet
cats asleep on the other couch
you are studying
The Basic Book of
     Organic Gardening
you say you have waited
all these years to
live this life
everything new now
outside our window
it is snowing
on snow
when it thaws and goes
it will be spring
and you will have
your earth to turn
our first summer garden
our new country life

7:05 P.M./21:11:72

this is the buddha hour
for cats:
Bujo contemplating on
the oriental rug
Sato in the other room
on the old pine floor;
running water means
dishes are being done,
well fed and writing
deer are moving now
outside our window,
one quarter moon—
who can name the conjunctions
of the heart

13:IV:72

april winter
mud/
white &
bone chill
we stop in
tire track ankle
water hollow
to hear first
bear hoots
of spring